I0519382

THE TWO SIDES
OF BEING SINGLE

WAYNE DRAYTON

THE TWO SIDES
OF BEING SINGLE

Copyright © 2023 by Wayne Drayton

All rights reserved. This book or any portion thereof may not be reproduced or used in any manner whatsoever without the express written permission of the publisher except for the use of brief quotation in a book review.

ISBN: 978-1-962363-25-9 (sc)
ISBN: 978-1-962363-26-6 (e)

Rev. date: 11/23/2023

CHAPTER 1

INTRODUCTION

Ever since I was thirteen years old and growing up in the church, I have been hearing a lot of people talk about getting married. In fact, some Christians believe that marriage is mandatory in order to be perfect Christians. In addition, they believe a Christian can be normal only by getting married and having children. Those who aren't married are somehow exiled by the body of Christ which is the church. They aren't called upon to participate in church activities because of being single. Not to put it in a bad way, marriage can be somewhat overrated, and I believe too much emphasis has been placed on this scared institution to the point that marriage could be a requirement for salvation.

But what most Christians don't realize is that God loves single Christians as well as married Christians. God is just and good to all people regardless of whatever marital status they may decide to partake in their lives. In 2 Chronicles 19:7, it states that "for there is no iniquity with the Lord our God, nor respect a person nor taking of gifts." We are free agents in the sight of God. God doesn't judge us according to our marital status, but He judges us according to our faith. The Bible says, "But without faith it is impossible to please Him; for he that cometh to God must believe that he is, and that he is a rewarder of them that diligently seek Him" (Heb. 11:6).

When Jesus Christ died on the cross for our sins and rose again, He bestowed His love on single Christians as well as married Christians who accept Him as Lord and Savior of their lives. Jesus came into the world to "save His people from their sins" (Matt. 1: 21). The blood He shed for us at Calvary is enough to redeem people from all of their sins. Also, His blood cleans us and makes us pure. As a result of His work on the cross, His grace and mercy is reserved for single and married people alike.

In this book, I will discuss two perspectives of being single by the Bible's point of view. First, I will discuss being single and remaining single. This perspective is rarely talked about in the church. When some people discuss singleness in the church, they don't talk about a lifetime of singleness; they refer to being single until a person finds a mate. But in order to remain single, a person will need God's assistance to maintain being single. A person cannot accomplish a lifetime of singleness on his or her own. Second, I will discuss being single and waiting for the Lord to bless a person with a mate. This perspective is the one that is partaken by most Christians. It is of vital importance that Christians should marry the person that God has ordained for them to marry. He knows exactly who a person should marry. Therefore, a person should wait on the Lord and trust Him to bless that person with the mate. Finally, I will conclude the book with an invitation for the reader to accept Christ as one's personal savior and Lord. It doesn't matter what marital status one takes in this life; what matters is where a person is going to spend eternity when a person dies. Jesus told Nicodemus, "Verily, verily, I say unto thee, Except a man be born again he cannot see the kingdom of God" (John 3:3).

Furthermore, a person can be officially single only once in his or her lifetime. When a person gets married, the single life comes to an end. However, if the marriage ends in divorce, the person is no longer single because that person was married before. A person also isn't single if a person's mate is deceased. That person is considered to be a widower. A person can only be single if a person has never been married. Also, if a person is separated and awaiting divorce, the person's marital status then becomes separated.

CHAPTER 2

SINGLENESS DOESN'T MEAN TO BE ALONE

The one main fact that Christians should realize is that being single and being alone are different from one another. Being alone means getting apart from others. A person purposely isolates himself or herself from other people. Normally, this is due to a person suffering from severe depression and having low self-esteem. Also, a person may want to be alone because that person believes no one cares about him or her. However, being single means to be a standout and to be unique from others. As far as marital status goes, being single means never having been married. It is important for Christians to make the distinction between being alone and being single because they could mistakenly classify a person as being alone when they are really being single and vice versa.

A scripture in the Bible that is mistakenly used by some Christians to justify getting married but not remaining single is Genesis 2:18. Some Christians misquote this scripture by saying, "It is not good for man to be alone." But one must look at this scripture carefully. The exact quote of the scripture is, And the Lord said, "It is not good that the man should be alone. I will make him a help meet for him." The man referred to in this scripture is Adam. That helpmeet in the scripture turned out to be his wife Eve.

But God saw the glory that men gave Him so He decided to make more men upon the earth to worship and praise the Lord. This would be done through the process of reproduction. Also, Christians are supposed to be married before having sex; this scripture is not talking about getting married. Both men and women have been given the power to create a child through reproduction. In fact, the establishment of Adam and Eve reproducing will eventually lead to the birth of our Lord and Savior Jesus in that Jesus must be born in human flesh to show humans how to live for God. But Jesus's birth will happen as a result of the Holy Spirit impregnating Mary by his power.

The apostle Paul discusses the gift of singleness in 1 Corinthians 7:8–9. It states that "I say therefore to the unmarried and widows. It is good for them if they abide even as I. But if they cannot contain let them marry; for it is better to marry than to burn." He wished that the saints in the Corinthians church could live the single life like Him, but He realized that everyone doesn't have the gift to be single because a person can't maintain his or her sexual desires. Therefore, the apostle Paul told the Corinthian church to go ahead and get married, but the individual must keep in mind that sex isn't the main objective in marriage. When a Christian decides to be single, he or she has the freedom to serve the Lord. The apostle Paul says in 1 Corinthians 7:32, "But I would have you without carefulness. He that is unmarried careth for the things that belong to the Lord, how he may please the Lord." A single person can concentrate on serving God fully and freely so that a person can have an intimate relationship with God. By being single, a Christian won't be distracted by the cares of this world. In addition, a person can easily hear the voice of God revealing His will.

A single Christian, as a result of the freedom a person has in his or her unmarried status, can make God a number one priority in a Christian's life. Jesus says, "But seek ye first the kingdom of God and His righteous, and all these things shall be added unto you" (Matt. 6:33). A person must remember that before we came to God for salvation through Jesus Christ, God showed His love to us when we were still in our sinful state. In Romans 5:8, it says, "But God commendeth his love toward us, in that, while we were sinners, Christ died for us." Because Jesus Christ put us first by dying on the cross for our sins over two thousand years ago, we should put Him first in our lives every day. By putting God first in our lives, everything in the life of the believer will fall in its rightful place.

Although being alone may not be good for some people, there are times in a Christian's life in which he or she needs to spend some solitary time with God. Reading God's word helps a Christian understand His will and live according to it. This will prevent a Christian from believing in false doctrine. Also, it is imperative that a single Christian has a constant prayer life in this world. Satan will try to tempt single Christians if they don't pray and ask God not to lead them into temptation. But as long as Christians put their faith in God, God isn't going to leave His people alone to battle Satan.

CHAPTER 3

DON'T BE FRUSTRATED ABOUT
BEING SINGLE

Some Christians become frustrated because God hasn't blessed them with a mate, and they believe that marriage is a cure to their loneliness. As a result, single Christians hurry to find their mate without consulting God for guidance through the Holy Spirit. But when it comes to being a single Christian, God doesn't want a single Christian to be in a desperate state of mind in his or her singleness. He wants single Christians to be at peace while they choose to be single.

Having peace with God is important to a single Christian. It brings calm in such a way that a single Christian can appreciate being unique and not having to be worried about being married. God will send this peace "which passeth all understanding shall keep your hearts and minds through Christ Jesus" (Phil. 4:6). By God sending his inner peace in the hearts of believers through Jesus Christ, single Christians won't go through any anxieties about being single. God's peace is beyond man's comprehension and can reside in the heart of the believer to enjoy the single life. While the world may be in a mad rush to find the perfect mate, a single Christian can rest easy knowing God will keep that person by his Holy Spirit, living in the individual.

A single Christian has a friend in God. A single Christian doesn't have to be alone in this world because God is always there to help His people in need. God says, "I will never leave thee nor forsake thee" (Heb 13:5). Since God is a friend to Christians, He gives insight into His will for His people. Jesus says, "Hence forth, I call you not servants; for the servant knoweth not what his lord doeth; but I call you friends; for all things that I have heard of my Father I have make know unto you"(John 15:15). Jesus wanted His people to know that He was going to have an intimate relationship with God through the Holy Spirit although He was going to heaven to be with his Father, God. One day, if Christians remain faithful to his will, Jesus says, "In my Father's house are many mansions; if it were not so, I would have told you. I go to prepare a place for you. And if I go and prepare a place for you, I will come again and receive you unto myself; that where I am, there ye may be also" (John 14:2–3).

Single Christians shouldn't get upset when people around them decide to get married. Instead of being frustrated because they are not married to anyone, single Christians should be celebrating the sacred institution of marriage. Christians must keep in mind that God created marriage for mankind through the union of Adam and Eve, according to Genesis 2:21–24. In these scriptures, God put Adam to sleep, took one of His ribs, put it in Eve, and the two of them became one flesh in God's sight. God concluded creating marriage through Adam and Eve by saying, "Therefore shall a man leave his father and his mother and shall cleave unto his wife, and they shall be one flesh" (Gen. 2:24). The man must be the one to leave home and marry his wife and take her into his home. The husband lays down the foundation for the marriage since God ordained him to be the leader of the home.

Another reason marriage should be celebrated by single Christians and not be the source of frustration for them is that marriage is symbolic of the relationship between Christ and the church. In this relationship, the husband is symbolic of Christ while the wife is symbolic of the church. According to Ephesians 5:22–24, the apostle Paul says wives should submit to their husbands because the "husband is the head of the wife, even as Christ is the head of the church: and He is savior of the body. Therefore as the church is subject unto Christ, so let the wives be to their own husbands in everything." But the husband must not mistreat their wives. Apostle Paul urged husbands to love their wives even as Christ loves the church and has given himself for it (Eph. 5:25). The wife shouldn't be forced to submit to her husband. It must be voluntary on her part, and she must place her trust willingly and freely under her husband's care.

In addition, single Christians can avoid frustration about not being married by loving God with their whole hearts which are their innermost beings. When Jesus Christ was asked by a lawyer, "Master, which is the greatest commandment?" (Matt. 22:36), Jesus replied, "Thou shalt love the Lord with all thy heart, and with all thy soul and with all thy mind. This is the first and great commandment" (Matt. 22:37–38). With God coming into the heart of a believer, the believer can obey God and perform His will.

Also, not only can a single Christian show one's love for God but a single Christian can also show his or her love for other people. Jesus says the second commandment is "Thou shalt love thy neighbor as thyself" (Matt. 22:39). In order to love all people, regardless of race, religion, or gender, a person must first love himself or herself. Once people see the love believers have toward God and other people, they will be inspired to accept Christ as their Lord and Savior.

In summary, single Christians need not be frustrated about being single because they don't have to go through the pressure of trying to maintain a marriage and raise children. They can live a life free of stress. Again, there is nothing wrong with getting married. But a person must be prepared for marriage. If a person is not ready for marriage, then a person should enjoy the single life until he or she is ready to get married, or the person can choose to remain single.

CHAPTER 4

Enjoy the Single Life

The single life needs to be cherished by Christians. As stated before, a person can be officially single only once in his or her lifetime. This should be a time to accomplish one's goal such as getting an education and having a career. Now a person can reach these goals while a person is married. But a person would need to focus on one's marriage as well as on trying to accomplish a person's goals. If people would focus more on their goals than on their marriage, this could put added pressure to the marriage. Having children can also be a distraction from completing one's goals. Therefore, Christians should take advantage of being single to evaluate themselves to determine whether or not they want to stay single or get married.

The main focus of the single life of a Christian is to serve the Lord. One of the ways Christians can serve the Lord is to minister to other people. Jesus says that ministering to other people is one way of serving Him. He stressed this in the book of Matthew 25:32–46. In these scriptures, Jesus addressed helping people who are in need, such as those who are naked, hungry, and thirsty. If a Christian meets the needs of these people, God will reward them for their faithfulness and they can enter into heaven. But if a Christian doesn't meet the needs of these people, then God will sentence them to "eternal damnation." Single Christians have the best chance to volunteer their time to help people in need because they have plenty of freedom and time to devote their efforts to the needy. In addition, they aren't tied down by marriage and they can give all of their attention to helping people in need.

If a single Christian wants to get married, the single life would allow an individual Christian to build a good foundation for an individual Christian to be a good mate. A single Christian needs to check his or her strengths and weaknesses concerning one's ability to be a good spouse. A single Christian should enhance one's strengths and integrate them into the marriage to make the marriage work. As for the weaknesses, a single Christian needs to take note of them and correct these weaknesses before one gets married. It is imperative that a single Christian understands marriage before getting married. Proverbs 24:27 states, "Prepare thy work without, and make it fit for thyself in the field, and afterwards build thine house." In other words, know and understand marriage before getting involved in it.

The single life gives a single Christian the opportunity to examine oneself spiritually. If single Christians don't take the time to examine their faith in God daily, then Satan could easily deceive them and put them in a lost state. The apostle Paul says, "Examine yourselves, whether ye be in the faith. Prove your own selves. Know ye not your own selves, how that Jesus Christ is in you, except ye be reprobated?" (2 Cor. 13:5). A reprobate is an unworthy person who doesn't have morals. By examining oneself every day, a single Christian can see his or her shortcomings and ask God to put him or her on the right path that leads to God and His righteousness. Reading and performing God's word every day assist a person searching his or her spirit to determine if he or she is still maintaining his or her faith in God.

A single Christian needs to take care of his or her body physically so that he or she can worship and praise God. Proper diet and exercise help keep the body performing the will of God and lengthen one's days on the earth. The apostle Paul says, "I beseech you therefore by the mercies of God, that ye present your bodies a living sacrifice, holy, acceptable unto God, which is your reasonable service" (Rom. 12:1). The purpose for creating men on earth is so that man can recognize God and serve Him. Since God is responsible for man's creation, man should glorify God for creating him and blessing him.

Not only does a single Christian need to be concerned about his or her physical well-being, but he or she must also be concerned about his or her mental health. Satan loves to attack the mind of the individual so he can deceive a single Christian into turning away from God and make him or her believe his lies. But God wants believers to have a ready-made mind to serve Him. The apostle Paul told Timothy, "For God hath not given us the spirit of fear; but of power, and of love, and of a sound mind" (2 Tim. 1:7). Christians must put on "the helmet of salvation" (Eph. 6:7) to prevent Satan from penetrating the mind of believers.

God can use single Christians as well as married Christians. Furthermore, single Christians can't go to hell for being single. God can use a single Christian for His glory and expect him or her to be great. Jesus Christ died and rose again to save everyone, including single Christians. They should never be left out of church activities because they are always available to lend a helping hand. Therefore, if Christians are not married, they should appreciate being single and enjoy the single life.

CHAPTER 5

CONTROLLING ONE'S SEXUAL DESIRE WHILE BEING SINGLE

One of the main objectives to maintaining a single life is controlling one's sexual desires. God created humans to be sexual beings. Sex was created for a man to be attracted to a woman and for a woman to be attracted to a man. God installed these desires for the purpose of reproduction in marriage. Hebrews 13:4 states that "Marriage is honorable in all, and the bed undefiled; but whore-mongers and adulterers God will judge." Although it may be hard to maintain a single life, it is possible to do it with self-control and with faith in God. A single Christian has to avoid lust in his or heart. Lust causes a saint to be distracted from serving God. This is why God said in the Ten Commandments "Thou shall not covet" (Exod. 20:17). Jesus took lusting in the heart to a deeper level. He says, "That whosoever looketh on a woman to lust after her committed adultery with her already in his heart" (Matt. 5:28). Deuteronomy 24:1–2 made it easy for a husband to divorce his wife by finding any uncleanness in his wife and allowing him to divorce his wife and marry someone else.

But Jesus demonstrated that a man can also be found guilty of adultery by having lust in his heart for another woman.

Satan will try His best to tempt a single Christian to commit fornication. He puts lust in a believer's heart so that believer not only loses one's virginity but also loses his or her relationship with God. But God won't allow Satan to distract the believer to be deceived. He will protect the believer's heart from Satan's penetrating power as Satan tries to make a believer lose his fellowship with God. Saints will always get the victory over Satan by following the scripture found in James 4:7 which says, "Submit yourselves therefore to God. Resist the devil, and He will flee from you."

God's Holy Spirit plays a role in controlling a single Christian's sexual desires. The Holy Spirit is a keeper and protector of the believer's heart. The Holy Spirit is a teacher to saints as well. Jesus says, "But the comforter, which is the Holy Ghost, whom the Father will send in my name, He shall teach you all things, and brings all things to your remembrance, whatsoever I have said unto you" (John 14:26). The Holy Spirt is a living person who resides in the believer's heart, not some inanimate object. The Apostle Paul says, "For as many as are led by the Spirit of God, they are the sons of God" (Rom. 8:14).

Another way for single Christians to control their sexual desires is to meditate on God's word. Dwelling on God's word brings delight to the believer. If the believer meditates on God's word, sex won't overwhelm the believer's heart. King David says, "But his delight is the law of the Lord; and his law doth he meditate day and night" (Ps. 1:2). By pondering on God's word, single Christians can focus on performing God's will.

Most people control their sexual desires by the process of masturbation and orgasm—masturbating for men and orgasm for women. The Bible is somewhat silent on these processes, but there is a scripture that addresses the process of masturbation. Genesis 38:8–10 points out masturbation on the part of Onan, the son of Judah. Onan was involved in a levirate marriage which states that a dead man's brother takes over the marital duties of his decease brother and father a son who would assume his decease father's inheritance. If a brother dies and marries a wife with children, then the brother who is the next oldest to his deceased brother takes responsibility of his deceased brother's wife and children in the name of his deceased brother. If Onan has any children with his deceased brother's wife, the children will be raised in his decease brother's name. Onan decided to masturbate his sperm on the ground so that he won't raise children in his deceased brother's name. When God saw what Onan was doing, he decided to punish him for not wanting to raise his deceased brother's children. Although orgasm isn't mentioned in the Bible, it has the same purpose as masturbation, which is to fulfill one's sexual lust.

God doesn't want His people to have a burning desire to have sex, although God did create humans to have sexual desire to be attracted to the opposite sex. If a single Christian has a burning desire to have sex with someone, he or she will not be able to praise and worship God effectively. The apostle Paul offers a remedy for someone having a burning desire to have sex. He says, "But if they cannot contain, let them marry; for it is better to marry than to burn" (1 Cor. 7:9). Marriage is a sacred institution created by God to avoid fornication. However, a person has to keep in mind that having sex isn't the main objective in marriage. There are other things to consider in marriage besides having sex such as paying bills and having daily devotion to God in the home.

Controlling one's sexual desire will cause a man to have fewer wet dreams while he sleeps at night. Wet dreams are erotic dreams that are accompanied by ejaculation. In order to control these wet dreams, a person must read and study God's word and have His word in his or her heart. Also, single Christians should put on "the helmet of salvation" (Eph. 6:7) in order to protect their minds from any illicit sexual desires while they are sleeping at night. Also, a single Christian can read a scripture from God's word before going to sleep so that a single Christian's meditation will not be on those illicit sexual desires, but it will be on God's word.

Some people enjoy watching pornographic movies and reading pornographic magazines as a means of attempting to control their sexual desires. But doing either one of these won't control their sexual desires. They will increase their sexual desires to a boiling point. Single Christians should not have anything to do with pornography whether it is reading a magazine or watching it on television or seeing it on a video or a movie.

While pornography is a billion-dollar business, single Christians should never put themselves in a vulnerable position by allowing themselves to view any form of pornography so they won't fall into any temptation by Satan. Jesus says, "And if thy rise right eye offends thee, pluck it out, and cast it from thee; for it is profitable for thee that one of thy members should perish, and not that thy whole body should be cast into hell" (Matt. 5:29). Jesus wasn't telling His listeners to literally pull out their eyes. He was telling them to control their eyes spiritually so that they won't be distracted by anything that appears to be evil. In this way, a single Christian's body won't be cast into hell by God for watching evil things like pornography.

A person doesn't have to remain single, but he or she can change his or her mind and decide to get married. If a person decides to get married instead of remaining single, then he or she hasn't done anything wrong. The apostle Paul says, "But and if thou marry, thou has not sinned; and if a virgin Mary, she has not sinned. Nevertheless such shall have trouble in the flesh; but I spare you" (1 Cor. 7:28). If a person changes his or her mind about being married, then one has to balance out his or her relationship with their mate and God, whereas God is first but the mate is second. It is imperative to marry a Christian so that he or she can understand this hierarchy in order for the marriage to stay together. He or she must love God as well as his or her mate. If a person puts God first and put his or her mate second, then he or she won't have "trouble in the flesh" (1 Cor. 7:28).

Furthermore, all marriages experience some type of problems. The issue is whether a husband and wife can maintain their relationship in the midst of these problems. These issues could be economic pressures like paying bills and staying out of debt. Also, political issues could come up concerning whom a person would vote to put that person in public office. If these issues are not dealt with when they occur in a marriage, they will disrupt a marriage and the marriage will end up in divorce. But in a

Christian marriage, God holds a marriage together, for Jesus says, "Wherefore they are no more twain, but one flesh. What therefore God hath joined together, let no man put asunder" (Matt. 19:6).

CHAPTER 6

BE AT PEACE IN YOUR SINGLE LIFE

For some single people, they worry about who is going to be right person for them to marry. They end up rushing into the world looking for their mate without consulting God and without getting to know the person to determine if he or she is the right person for them. But single Christians don't have to panic because they may not be blessed by God with a mate yet. They must realize that God takes his time to bless his people with their mates. However, single Christians can be at peace being single in the name of Jesus Christ.

Single Christians don't have to panic and worry about being single. God resides in their hearts, and He leaves them with a sense of calm. God knows how to take care of his people in their singleness. He doesn't want single Christians to worry about anything because he knows how to provide for them. Jesus says, "Therefore I say unto you, Take no thought for your life, what ye shall eat, or what ye shall drink: nor yet for your body, what ye shall put on. Is not the life more than meat and the body more than raiment?"(Matt. 6:25). Jesus holds his people near and dear to his heart. The single Christian should know that they have value with God through his precious son, Jesus Christ. God values the world so much that He gave his son Jesus on the cross so that if anyone believes on Him, he or she will obtain eternal life (John 3:16).

The Holy Spirit lives in the heart of the Christian. He speaks peace to the hearts of His saints. He is a guide and a teacher to the believers. Jesus says, "But the comforter, which is the Holy Ghost, whom the Father will send in my name he shall teach you all things, and bring all things to your remembrance, whatsoever I have said unto you" (John 14:26). Jesus knew that believers were going to need someone to sustain them while He goes to take his place on the right side of his Father, God. Single Christians should listen to the Holy Spirit in order to find out what God's will is for their lives.

In order for the Holy Spirit to operate in a Christian's life, a Christian must be led by the Holy Spirit. This shows God that a Christian belongs to Him and he or she desires God's will to be done in one's life. The apostle Paul says, "But ye are not in the flesh, but in the Spirit, if so be that the Spirit of God dwell in you. Now if any man have not the spirit of God, he is none of His" (Rom. 8:9). The Holy Spirit lives in the hearts of believers, leading them into all truth about God's word. The apostle Paul added, "For as many as are led by the Spirit of God, they are the sons of God" (Rom. 8:14). Staying in God's Spirit helps maintain our faith and peace with him in our single Christian life while other single people worry about finding their "Mr. or Mrs. Right."

But single Christians need not panic or worry about finding "Mr. or Mrs. Right." God's peace will abide in a Christian's heart so that a Christian can remain calm and feel good about the single life. The world may experience anxiety about being single, but single Christians can place their trust in God to keep them in perfect peace while they are single. The apostle Paul says, "And the peace of God which passeth all understanding shall keep your hearts and minds through Christ Jesus" (Phil. 4:7). God's peace goes beyond human understanding and can't be comprehended by the flesh. The world's peace is temporary, but God's peace is eternal. His peace is able to keep believers calm through the presence of Jesus Christ in His name and His authority.

The world doesn't think of having peace the way a Christian does. The world's peace is contingent on a temporary peace that may or may not occur. The world's peace is made, but it doesn't last a long time. Unlike the world's peace, God's peace is everlasting when single Christians place their faith in God. As a result, Christians can rest assured that God will reside in their hearts and give them the peace they need to sustain them. Jesus says, "Peace I leave with you, my peace I give unto you: not as the world giveth, give I unto you. Let not your heart be trouble, neither let it be afraid" (John 14:27).

Whenever a single Christian has to deal with the anxieties of this life, God will take care of him or her. Christians can always come to God to get their issues resolved by Him. First Peter 5:6–7 states, "Humble yourselves therefore under the mighty hand of God, that He may exalt you in due time: Casting all your care upon him; for He careth for you." God knows how to take care of his people who trust Him and His will. But if a person is not humble before God, God will bring him or her down. "Pride goeth before destruction, and a haughty spirit before a fall" (Prov. 16:18).

A single Christian is never alone while being single. God will be a help to him or her in the time of trouble. God will be a refuge and a protection to single Christians. King David wrote in Psalms 57:1, "Be merciful unto me, O God, be merciful unto me: for my soul trusteth in thee; yea, in the shadow of thy wings will I make my refuge, until these calamities be overpast." Like David, God will deliver single Christians out of all their trials and tribulations. He will protect His saints until all of their troubles are pass over them.

CHAPTER 7

GOD WILL NEVER FORSAKE SINGLE CHRISTIANS

Single Christians must keep in mind that God hasn't forgotten about them. He doesn't want his people in darkness, but He wants them to walk in the light of his son Jesus Christ. They need to rely on God when they feel alone. God will lift them up and keep them like a parent who cares for his or her child. He knows everything about individuals. King David says, "Thou knowest my downsitting and mine uprising, thou understandest my thought afar off" (Ps. 139:2). There is absolutely nothing about a human being that God doesn't know about him or her.

God is the creator of mankind and all of creation. When God created man, He created man in his image. Since He created both men and women, they are both considered equals in His sight. Genesis 1:28 states, "And God blessed them, and God said unto them, Be fruitful and multiply, and replenish the earth, and subdue it: and have dominion over the fowl of the air, and every living thing that moveth upon the earth." He created men and women for the purpose of reproduction if they choose to reproduce and have children, for humans are free agents in God's sight. Because God has created man to take care of the earth, He wants man to give glory to Him.

Single Christians need to be led by the Holy Spirit so that God can help them in their time of trials and tribulations as long as they abide on the earth. But God can help a Christian obtain victory over his or her trial and tribulation. "For whatsoever is born of God overcometh the world: and this is the victory that overcometh the world, even our faith. Who is he that overcometh the world, but he that believeth that Jesus is the Son of God?" (1 John 5:4–5). God desires for his people to be victorious and to be successful in this life. With God's help, Christians can overcome anything in Jesus's name.

As Christians grow in maturity, God will always be there for His saints. He will never forsake believers because of their age. As King David says, "I have been young, and now am old; yet have I not seen the righteous forsaken, nor His seed begging bread" (Ps. 37:25). No matter how young or old a person becomes in God's sight, He won't forsake him or her in this evil world. In addition, God will not leave His people in a needy state of mind. As long as single Christians stay faithful to God, God will provide for His saints.

One of the most powerful scriptures in the Bible that demonstrates that God won't forsake not only single Christians but also anybody that lives on earth is John 3:16. It states, "For God so loved the world, that he gave His only begotten son, that whosoever believes on Him should not perish but have everlasting life." Everybody in this world, including single Christians, has the potential of obtaining salvation through Jesus Christ. When Jesus did his work on the cross, He died and rose again for single people as well as married people.

God will not allow Satan to attack believers more than they can handle. Satan can't arbitrarily attack God's people without His permission. Job, for example, was attacked by Satan due to God giving Job over to Satan. But because of Job's patience, waiting for His change to come, Job was blessed by God with a double blessing. God will see his people through all of the tough times that may occur in their lives. The apostle Paul says, "There hath not temptation taken you but such as is common to man; but God is faithful, who will not suffer you to be tempted above that ye are able; but will with the temptation also make a way to escape, that ye may able to bear it" (1 Corinthians 10:13). God doesn't tempt His people, but he tests their loyalty and faith toward Him. For every type of temptation, God has an escape route to get out of it. No one in this world is exempt from being in a difficult trial because this world is not perfect.

Right now, Jesus Christ is currently sitting at the right hand of God. He is praying for believers in heaven while they are living in this world. When Jesus rose again, He took his rightful place on his throne which is on the right hand–side of his father, God. The apostle Paul says, "Who is He that condemneth? It is Christ that died, yea rather, that is risen again, who is even at the right hand of God, who also maketh intercession for us" (Rom. 8:34). Jesus is constantly praying for His saints twenty-four hours a day and seven days a week.

Not only is Jesus making intercessions for believers, but the Holy Spirit is making intercessions for believers also. Christians may not know what to say as they are making their request to God. The Holy Spirit will articulate a prayer request and will relay the prayer back to God the Father. The apostle Paul says, "Likewise the Spirit also helpeth our infirmities; for we know not what we should pray for as we ought; but the Spirit itself maketh intercession for us with groanings which cannot be uttered" (Rom. 8:26) The Holy Spirit lives in the heart of believers, revealing the will of God. He knows what saints need from God, and he knows what to say to God through Jesus Christ.

God loves his people and will give his people victory over the enemy who is Satan. Satan will try to discourage God's people by attempting to deceive them. But Christians must take heed that Satan knows the truth of God's word and turns it into a lie. This was evident with the fall of man. When Satan deceived Eve in eating the fruit of the tree of the knowledge of good and evil, she gave the fruit to her husband Adam and he ate it. As a result, sin entered into the world. But Jesus Christ, after performing His work on the cross, offers the sinners forgiveness and cleanliness of their sins through His blood, death, and resurrection.

CHAPTER 8

STAYING ON ONE'S KNEES IN PRAYER

If a Christian wants to live a single lifestyle, he or she should ask God for guidance. The single life isn't an easy life for a Christian to live. A Christian has to contend with sexual desires, knowing that God created men to be sexual beings who are given the power of reproduction (Gen. 1:27–28). But if Christians desire to be single, they need to stay on their knees and pray to God to contain them so they could serve the Lord without being distracted. A single Christian can't control his or her sexual desires on his or her own. Single Christians definitely must have God's help to control their sexual desires by prayer since God is the one who installed those desire in them in the first place.

To deal with God in prayer, one must have faith in Him. By having faith in God, a single Christian is rendering his or her life for God's use. The apostle Paul says, "I beseech you therefore, brethren, by the mercies of God that ye present your bodies, a living sacrifice, holy and acceptable unto God, which is your reasonable service" (Rom. 12:1). A single Christian must submit to God in such a way that he or she will have God actively in his or her life. It is only by God's mercy and grace that single Christians are able to surrender themselves to God and be used by Him.

Staying humble before God in prayer is the key for God to exalt single Christians. Humility means taking on a lower status in order to be lifted up by a certain authority. By being humble before God, He will promote Christians who are single to certain positions in life. They are exalted by God only because he is going to be the one doing the promoting. Being humble is an attitude all Christians should possess. Jesus says, "Blessed are the meek; for they shall inherit the earth" (Matt. 5:5). A single Christian can come to greatness by his or her meekness toward God while being used by God.

Single Christians should never believe they can have a single lifestyle without God's help. This could cause a single Christian to develop pride in his or her heart. This attitude disrupts a single Christian from being humble before God. If single Christians try to be single without God, they will be easily tempted by Satan to commit fornication and have lust in their hearts. Single Christians must remember that "pride goeth before destruction and a haughty spirit before a fall" (Prov. 16:18). God won't allow anyone or anything to get ahead of Him. God said in the Ten Commandments, "Thou shalt have no other gods before me" (Exod. 20:3). Exodus 20:5 describes God as "jealous" of those who worship other gods.

It is very important for single Christians to keep in mind that God only hears the prayers of the righteous. If single Christians make their prayer requests to God, and they are righteous before God, He will hear their prayers that are rendered to Him. The apostle James says, "The effectual fervent prayer of a righteous man availeth much" (James 5:16). The Christian's intense prayer to God produces wonderful results.

When a single Christian doubts God in granting his or her request in prayer, God won't respond to that prayer. A single Christian may pray to God, but he or she is not sure that God will hear a prayer; in addition, one may not be sure if God is going to answer a prayer. But James described this type of faith as "wavering." James says, "But let Him ask in faith, nothing wavering. For He that waverth is like a wave of the sea driven with the wind and tossed. For let not that man thinks he shall receive anything of the Lord" (James1:6–7). A Christian must be absolutely sure about his or her petition to God in that he will bring about his or her blessing.

Single Christians must be patient with God in getting their prayers answered according to God's will. Single Christians should never rush God in blessing them. He has a time set aside on his timetable to bless His people. God's timing and man's timing are different from one another. Moses prayed, "For a thousand years in thysight are but yesterday when it is past, and a watch in the night" (Ps. 90:4). Believers must be sensitive to God's timing so that they will know when He is operating in their lives.

Above all, single Christians should stay on their knees so that Satan will not tempt them into committing some form of fornication, or He could put lust in their hearts to satisfy their sexual desires. Praying will help single Christians maintain their sexual desires in order not to burn with passions. Single Christians must serve the Lord freely and willingly. God will not force his will on His saints, but rather, He would allow his people to make their own decisions to serve him. Prayer is the key in turning Satan away from tempting His saints.

CHAPTER 9

DON'T REGRET BEING SINGLE

Now, it's not the time to be depressed about being a single Christian. He or she may have this feeling because they can't find the right person to marry. They may not have the patience to wait on the Lord to bless them with a husband or a wife. Therefore, they either rush to find a husband or a wife without taking the time to know the person, or they become sad and alone, thinking no one cares about them. But God doesn't want single Christians to feel this way. He knows how to bring security to a single Christian's life.

A single Christian is never alone in God's sight. He knows where his people are located throughout the world. He never allows his people to walk in darkness. Jesus will shine his light out of the darkness so a single Christian can see his or her way clearly. In turn, because Jesus is the light and Christians can follow him, they become light as well. Jesus says, "Ye are the light of the world. A city that is set on an hill cannot be hid" (Matt. 5:14). God will stand with His people in good times and in bad times.

God knows how to provide for his people when they are in need of a blessing from him. All they have to do is trust Him to meet their needs. They need not worry about anything because God can help his people. The apostle Paul says, "But my God shall supply all your need according to his riches in glory by Christ

Jesus" (Phil. 4:19). Jesus said that God knows what a Christian needs before he or she asks him (Matt. 6:8).

Sometimes, a single Christian may believe that he or she can't maintain a single life because that person assume that marriage is mandatory and it is something that needs to be done in order to be perfect in God's sight. Jesus says, "Be ye therefore perfect, even as your Father which is in heaven is perfect" (Matt. 5:48). Accepting Jesus as Lord and Savior by faith results in a Christian being perfect, not marriage. A person doesn't have to get married in order to be a perfect Christian. What Jesus Christ performed on the cross is sufficient for a person to obtain perfection.

Also, God, through his Son Jesus Christ, can help a person maintain the single life. What a single Christian must do is rely on God's power and His will to take control of his or her life. Some single Christians may doubt that God can help them to be single because of their marital status. However, as Gabriel the archangel told Mary, "For with God nothing shall be impossible" (Luke 1:37). God will help single Christians control their sexual desires in order to remain single. If single Christians can declare as the Apostle Paul says, "I can do all things through Christ which strengthen me" (Phil. 4:13), then God will place his Holy Spirit in the believer to control his or her sexual desires in order to worship the Lord.

Single Christians should feel good about being married because God created marriage for mankind if they decide to exercise this option. Everything that God has created in this world, including marriage, is good in His sight. Therefore, single Christians should never say anything negative about marriage. Hebrews 13:4 says, "Marriage is honorable in all and the bed undefiled; but whoremongers and adulterers God will judge." Marriage is a sacred institution that consists of a lifetime commitment between a husband and a wife. Jesus says, "What therefore God hath joined together, let no man put asunder" (Matt. 19:6). Although the divorce rate may be higher in this world, marriage is still holy and acceptable.

CHAPTER 10

GIVING ONE'S SINGLE LIFE TO GOD

To remain single in God's sight, a single Christian must dedicate his or her single life to God. Sexual desires can be kept at bay by giving those desires to God for control. God is the one who is responsible for giving sexual desires to man. Therefore, God can suppress the sexual desire of a single Christian so that he or she can praise and worship God effectively. Surrendering to God's will to control one's sexual desire makes it easy for a single Christian to serve the Lord.

For one thing, a single Christian must make up his or her mind to dedicate his or her life to God. Once a single Christian makes up his or her mind to be single, Satan can't tempt single Christians to commit fornication which is forbidden by the word of God. The apostle Paul says, "For this is the will of God, even your sanctification, that ye should abstain from fornication; that every one of you should know how to possess his vessel in sanctification and honor" (1 Thes. 4:3-4). It is God's will for his people to stay away from sexual sins so that they can be made holy by the Holy Spirit.

The inner man of a single Christian should be given to God so that a single Christian can allow God's spirit to live in him or her, and the inner man can be protected from Satan by God's power. There is a constant battle between the flesh and the Holy Spirit.

Whereas the flesh causes a single Christian to commit sexual sins, the Holy Spirit strives to suppress those desires. The apostle Paul puts it this way: "For the flesh lusteth against the Spirit, and the Spirit against the flesh; and these are contrary the one to the other: so that ye cannot do the things that ye would" (Gal. 5:17). In this battle, a single Christian must choose which one he or she is going to serve: the flesh or the Holy Spirit. Jesus says, "No man can serve two masters; for either he will hate the one, and love the other; or else he will hold to the one, and despise the other. Ye cannot serve God and mammon" (Matt. 6:24). Christians are created by God to be free agents in his sight, and they need to make a decision whether to serve God or to serve the flesh.

A single Christian should strive to surrender his or her heart to the Lord. Single Christians need to give everything to the Lord. What is inside of a person's heart will eventually come to the outside for all the world to see. Jesus says, "Thou shalt love the Lord thy God with all thy heart, and with all thy soul, and with all thy mind" (Matt. 22:37). To protect the heart, a single Christian needs to put on "the breastplate of righteousness" (Eph. 6:14) which surrounds the heart for protection from the attacks of Satan.

God shows compassion to single Christians when they want to be single. He cares for them and shows them love unlike any other person this world. He won't allow Satan to tempt His people to commit fornication. The devil is going to make it hard for single Christians to maintain a single life. But God can help single Christians overcome the temptations of the devil if single Christians stay in the word of God and pray that, God help them maintain a single life.

A single Christian needs to establish a strong prayer life before God. Giving oneself to daily prayer helps in dedicating one's life to the Lord. The constant prayer of a saint is like incense going up before God. Jesus says, "Ask, and it shall be given you; seek and ye shall find; knock, and it shall be opened unto you; for everyone that asketh receiveth and He that seeketh findeth; and to Him that knocketh it shall be opened" (Matt. 7:7–8). God will always answer the prayer of saints once they render their requests to Him.

CHAPTER 11

SOME BIBLICAL CHARACTERS WHO WERE SINGLE

There are Bible characters who lived the single life in the scriptures. They focused on the Lord and placed their faith in God. God would show visions about His will to his people. He spoke to them directly and publicly. It was their faithfulness to God that made a difference for God to use them, not their marital status. In addition, these single people were obedient to God, regardless of their trying circumstances and difficulties.

Elijah was used by God while he resided most of his life in the desert as he prophesied in the northern kingdom of Israel. He stood before King Ahab to warn him that there would be no rain until he declared it (1 Kgs. 17:1). He challenged the four hundred and fifty Baal prophets at Mount Carmel to determine which god would rain fire from heaven (1 Kgs. 18:19–40). When Elijah called on God and fire came down, He ordered the Baal prophets to be killed. Also, He ordered the drought to come to an end (1 Kgs. 18:41). Malachi prophesied that God would send Elijah the prophet before the coming "day of the Lord" (Mal. 4:5). This prophecy spoke of John the Baptist being the forerunner of Jesus Christ. Elijah also appeared with Moses in the high mountain during Jesus's transfiguration before he left to be with God. Peter wanted to make three tents to be built for Jesus, Moses, and Elijah (Matt. 17:4; Mark 9:5; Luke 9:33). The two witnesses, mentioned in Revelations 11:6, could be Moses and Elijah.

Another biblical character who lived the single life and was used by God was Elisha. Before he was carried away in a chariot, Elijah bestowed his power on him by Elisha taking up Elijah's mantle. Elisha parted the Jordan River with Elijah's mantle (2 Kgs. 2:12–14). After this, he turned bad water into good water (2 Kgs. 2:19–22). He helped a widow obtain a miraculous amount of precious oil to deliver her children from slavery (2 Kgs. 4:1–7). He turned bad pottage into something edible (2 Kgs. 4: 38–41). He also fed hundreds of men by multiplying limited resources (2 Kgs. 4:42–44), and he miraculously provided water for thirsting armies (2 Kgs. 3:13–22). He also made an iron ax float (2 Kgs. 6:5–7). Because the Shunummite woman and her husband opened up their homes to Elisha, Elisha prophesied that the barren Shunummite woman would be blessed with a son by the Lord. One day, while the son was working in the field with his father, he suffered from a heatstroke and died. The mother pleaded for the man of God to be found so her son could be healed. When Elisha was found, he gave her son the healing he needed (2 Kgs. 4:8–37). He also healed Naaman the leper and dealt with Gehazi's dishonestly (2 Kgs. 5:27) In addition, he helped Israel defeat the Syrian army by using the power of God to blind them (2 Kgs. 6:8-7:20).

Jeremiah was called by God to maintain a single life to proclaim judgment on Judah. God ordered him to live without marriage and family. God told Jeremiah, "Thou shalt not take thee a wife, neither shalt thou have sons or daughters in this place" (Jer. 16:2). His main concern was to preach repentance to Judah, and he told Judah to surrender to Babylon because Babylon was a part of God's judgment on Judah. Jeremiah will face difficulties preaching to Judah, but God still used him although the people rejected his message and put him in the dungeon.

Another Bible character who remained single before God was John the Baptist. He spent most of his life in the wilderness preaching repentance and preparing the way for Jesus Christ to save people from their sins. He began his ministry at the Jordan River in the fifteenth year of the reign of Tiberius Caesar (Luke 3:1– 3). He refers to the multitudes of the Jordan River as a "generation of vipers" (Luke 3:7). He also said that a person who has two coats should give to a person who has none; tax collectors were warned to collect no more than they are due; soldiers were told not to rob anyone and be content with their wages (Luke 3:10–14). Jesus praised John for being the greatest of the prophets (Matt. 11:11).

The apostle Paul ministered to different churches as a single individual. Before he became an apostle for Christ, Paul persecuted the Christian church because he believed in the law of Moses, not Christ Jesus (Acts 8:1–3). On his way to Damascus, Jesus shined his light that caused Paul to fall on the ground. This light caused him to be blind. Ananias met Paul and restored his sight. He said to Paul he would be a minister to the Gentiles. He received the Holy Ghost and was baptized (Acts 9:17-18). He went on three missionary journeys establishing churches and preaching the Gospel. He is considered to be the most influential person of the New Testament church.

The greatest person to live the single life in the Bible is Jesus Christ. He focused on doing God's will, and He didn't let anyone or anything distract him from going to the cross. He told his parents Mary and Joseph, "How is it that ye sought me? Wist ye not that I must be about my Father's business?" (Luke 2:49). His main goal was to die for the sins of mankind so that we can be forgiven and cleansed. Christians can now be joint heirs in Christ once they accept Him as Lord and Savior. The Apostle Paul states, "For ye are all the children of God by Christ Jesus. For as many of you have been baptized into Christ have to put on Christ." (Gal. 3:26–27).

These Bible characters demonstrate that by putting one's faith on God, God can make a difference in a person's life. The marital status of these characters didn't hinder them from serving God. Instead, it gave them the opportunity to serve the Lord without being distracted from doing his will. They are inspirational to Christians to be faithful to the Lord in spite of being single.

CHAPTER 12

MARRY A GOD-ORIENTED MATE

Now it's time to talk about the perspective of being single and waiting for God to bless a person with a husband or a wife. God has ordained an individual for each single Christian to marry. The issue is the person choosing to allow God to bless him or her with a mate. Keep in mind that God knows the designated mate ahead of time. So there is no need to babble in a prayer request to God. Jesus says, "But when ye pray, use not vain repetitions, as the heathen do: for they think that they shall be heard for their much speaking. Be not ye therefore like unto them: for your Father knoweth what things ye have need of, before ye ask Him" (Matt. 6:7–8).

In order to understand the significance of marriage, one must know its definition. Marriage is a union in which a man and a woman share a lifetime commitment to each other while their relationship to God comes first. God has to be the first priority in a marriage. Both the husband and the wife must put God first in their marriage and put their needs second. Jesus says, "But seek ye first the kingdom of God, and his righteousness, and all these things shall be added unto you" (Matt. 6:33).

God can bless a marriage with Him as the focal point; however, a Christian marriage could be strained if one person marries someone who is not Christian. The non-Christian could cause the Christian to compromise his or her faith because the non-Christian doesn't believe in God. The apostle Paul gives a remedy for this dilemma. In

1 Corinthians 7:12–15, the Apostle Paul stated that if a Christian in a marriage marries a non-Christian, then he or she should go ahead and marry him or her if the non-Christian can tolerate his or her Christian mate living for God. The reason the apostle Paul says this is because there is a possibility that the non-Christian could accept Jesus Christ as Lord and Savior by the lifestyle of the Christian. But if the non-Christian decides to leave the marriage due to his or her Christian mate's lifestyle or any other reason, then the Christian is under no obligation to remain married to the non-Christian. Therefore, the Christian is allowed to get remarried.

But what if both the husband and the wife are Christians? The apostle Paul recommends that Christians who are married have two options. If they get a divorce, he says, "Let not the wife depart from her husband" (1 Cor. 7:10). Divorce was never God's intention for mankind because Jesus says, "Wherefore they are no more twain, but one flesh. What therefore God hath joined together, let not man put us asunder" (Matt. 19:6). In this case, believers are told to either get a divorce or reconcile (1 Cor. 7:11). This is why a person should marry a God-ordained mate.

There are certain characters who allow God to help them find a mate to marry. Genesis 24 tells the story of Abraham's servant going into Abraham's hometown of Mesopotamia to look for a wife for his son, Isaac. The servant approached a well, and he prayed to God whatever maiden of the city of Mesopotamia gave him and his camels a drink of water by the well, she was going to be Isaac's wife. Before he was through praying to God, Rebecca came to the well and gave the servant and his camels a drink of water. Rebecca was the daughter of Bethuel, who was the nephew of Abraham. She turned out to be the wife of Isaac.

Ruth also married someone who was ordained by God. At first, she was a widow while she lived in Moab with her mother-in-law Naomi, who also had a husband who died in Moab. After staying in Moab temporarily, Naomi decided to go back to her hometown of Bethelem-Judah when the famine there was over. Ruth begged Naomi to go back to Bethelem-Judah to live there with her. While she was living in Bethelem-Judah, Ruth worked in the wheat fields of Boaz as a gleaner. When he met Ruth for the first time, he was moved to find out she came from her homeland of Moab to be a help to Naomi. As a result, Boaz decides to marry Ruth so that he can recover land from his deceased cousin Elimelech, who was Naomi's husband. But there was another cousin who was closer to Elimelech than Boaz so that Boaz couldn't recover the inheritance. However, this cousin didn't recover the inheritance because he already had an inheritance. Boaz not only married Ruth, but he also gained his deceased cousin's inheritance. God put Boaz and Ruth together through God's providence which is God's control over a situation according to his will.

God's providence was also evident in the book of Esther although his name wasn't mentioned in the book. King Xerxes of Persia got rid of his wife Queen Vashti because she wouldn't display her beauty during a banquet. Another queen was sought for the king, and a decree went throughout Persia. Mordecai, Esther's cousin, recommended Esther to be the next queen, but she didn't reveal she was Jewish as Mordecai told her. Mordecai didn't bow down to Haman, Persia's prime minister; in addition, Haman got angry and decided to get a decree from the king to kill Mordecai and all the Jews. When Esther heard this from Mordecai, she put her life on the line by entering the sacred court. The king to set up a banquet to kill Haman and his followers as a result of Esther telling the king about Haman's plot. Mordecai was rewarded by the king for protecting him. Since God loves the Jews, He ordained the marriage of Xertes and Esther to protect the Jews from Haman's plot.

One must remember to let the Holy Spirit lead him or her to the right mate. Marriage is meant to last forever in God's sight. If a Christian gets a divorce in the eyes of man, the marriage is over, but in the eyes of God, the marriage still exists. Jesus says, "And I say unto you, whosoever shall put away his wife, except it be for fornication, and shall marry another, committeth adultery; and whoso marrieth her which is put away commit adultery" (Matt. 19:9). Jesus wasn't trying to make a law; rather, he stressed that whether or not a couple is together, they're still married in God's eyes if the husband and the wife are Christians.

CHAPTER 13

BE PATIENT WITH GOD

A single Christian should never rush God in finding a mate. God is making a way for a single Christian to be blessed. He wants single Christians to be patient with him so that they will know His will. God knows what is best for a single Christian to have as far as choosing a mate is concerned. He created Eve for Adam in the Garden of Eden (Gen. 2:18-24). Single Christians can rest assure that God will bless them with a mate of his choosing without being impatient with him.

Sometimes, single Christians may find themselves worried about looking for the right mate. But they don't allow God to lead them, and as a result, they end up getting hurt for choosing the wrong mate. God doesn't want his people to worry about finding the right mate because He has the exact mate we need to have for a lifetime commitment. Jesus says, "Therefore, I say unto you, Take no thought for your life, what ye shall eat, or what ye shall drink; nor ye for your body, what ye shall put on. Is not the life more than meat, and the body than raiment?" (Matt. 6:25). When single Christians put their faith in God, they need not worry about God supplying them with the right mate.

In addition, faith in God helps single Christians become patient when looking for a mate. Single Christians may or may not understand how God is blessing them with the right mate, but faith in God places one's trust in Him so that single Christians won't lose focus on what is God's will for finding the right person to marry. Single Christians should continue to have faith in God although it may take a long time in blessing them with a companion to marry. Faith will help single Christians line up with God's timing.

Patience in God allows single Christians to wait on God. While the world makes its own effort to find a husband or wife, single Christians should anticipate hearing the voice of God. The world uses such methods as blind dates and the internet, which will be discussed later in the book. Isaiah 40:31 states, "But they that wait on the Lord shall renew their strength; they shall mount up with wings of eagles; they shall run, and not be weary; and they shall walk. and not faint." Regardless of what the world does as far as finding the right person to marry, single Christians can depend on God's Spirit to lead them to their husbands or wives.

To be led by the Holy Spirit, single Christians need to live in the spirit, meaning allowing the Holy Spirit to control their lives. The Holy Spirit operates differently with a man looking for a wife from a woman looking for a husband. The single Christian male should be searching for his wife and showing the initiative to propose marriage. On the other hand, the single Christian woman should wait for the man to approach her as the Holy Spirit ministers to her to determine if this is the right person to marry. The single Christian male must follow Proverbs 18:22 which states, "Whoso findeth a wife findeth a good thing and obtaineth favour of the Lord." The man must build the foundation for the marriage as Christ is the head of the church (Eph. 5:23). However, the apostle Paul says, "Husbands, love your wives even as Christ also loved the church, and gave himself for it." (Eph. 5:25). The single Christian, therefore, must be sensitive to the Holy Spirit's leadership when working for a mate.

A single Christian man and single Christian woman have to get to know each other before they get married. The world may try to rush single Christians into getting married before they are ready, but they need not take heed to the world rushing them because according to Jesus Christ, "If ye were of the world, the world would love his own; but because ye are not of the world, but I have chosen you out of the world, therefore the world hateth you" (John 15:19). God always has the best interest at heart for believers, not the world.

CHAPTER 14

STAY AWAY FROM THE INTERNET

The method that most single people are using to find the right mate for them in the twenty-first century is the internet. There is a tremendous reliance of the internet for people. Nearly half of the people in the United States and around the world depend on the internet to find a companion. But on the other hand, Christians shouldn't put their faith in the internet because God is wiser and smarter than the internet.

The believers should put their faith in God only. They know that God will answer their prayers because having faith in God is necessary to get their prayers answered. Hebrews 11:6 says, "But without faith is it possible to please him; for He that cometh to God must believe that he is, and that he is a rewarder of them who diligently seek him." Belief in God brings about plenty of blessings for God's people. The Lord wants his people to trust Him so that they can have an intimate relationship with him. The stronger faith a believer has, the closer he or she can get to God.

The internet doesn't have the infinite knowledge of a human being that God has. The internet is limited by the amount of information it obtains from people. People put in their information into an online dating service in the hope that the computer can match them with the right mate. However, God is omniscient, meaning He is all knowing. A person can't run or hide from God regardless of where he or she may go in this world because He knows where to find the individual. He is omnipresent, meaning He is everywhere in this world. In addition, God is omnipotent, meaning He is all-powerful. Nothing or no one in this world is equal to the power of God. Psalms 139 coveys God being all knowing, and Proverbs 15:3 coveys God being everywhere "beholding the evil and the good."

The internet's search is pertaining to the flesh, not God. When some single people go online to look for a mate, they look for someone who is pleasing to them, not to God. They put the internet ahead of God, who created the internet. But God won't settle for second best; He frowns upon anything believers worship and praise ahead of Him. God says, "Thou shall not bow down thyself to them, nor serve them; for I the Lord thy God am a jealous God" (Exod. 20:5). God has a right to be envious because He gave the world his son, Jesus on the cross in order to be saved and cleansed from its sins.

God desires his people to have complete trust in Him. A single Christian must allow God to work in his or her life in order to be blessed with the right mate. Single Christians must make a decision to either trust God completely or trust the internet completely. Proverbs 3:5–6 says, "Trust in the Lord with all thine heart; and lean not unto thine own understanding. In all thy ways acknowledge Him, and he shall direct thy paths." Sometimes, single people may use their own methods in finding the right mate, but God wants single Christians to acknowledge Him as they search for the right companion. Sacrificing oneself to be used by God in being blessed with the right mate will motivate believers to put their trust in God.

If a single Christian has a plan to find a mate, he or she shouldn't let the internet make decisions to determine his or her rightful companion. Single Christians must prepare their hearts to allow the Holy Spirit to lead them to their future husbands or wives. God uses a believer in his or her own environment so he or she won't feel alone. Proverbs 16:3 states, "Commit thy works unto the Lord, and thy thoughts shall be established." The Lord cares about the plans of his people. He doesn't want them to act without consulting him.

The internet is limited in its scope in finding the right person. It calculates what an individual puts into it, but a single Christian prays to God and makes his or her requests to God. Single Christians can have a mate by God's will if they turn to Him. Jesus says, "Ask, and it shall be given unto you; seek and ye shall find; knock, and it shall be opened" (Matt. 7:7–8). One may go on the internet and not get what he or she asks for. But God always gives a person what he or she desires according to His will.

Single Christians must keep in mind that the internet is an inanimate object that can't bless them with a mate, unlike God. It is a gamble to let the internet find a mate because it is based solely on luck. A person really isn't sure that going online is going to help him or her; but God, who rules this world, is described by Jesus as "a spirit and they that worship Him must worship Him in spirit and truth" (John 4:24). There is a Holy Trinity who governs believers: Father, Son, and the Holy Ghost. Therefore, a single Christian should be dependent on God rather than the internet.

CHAPTER 15

CHRISTIANS SHOULD MARRY CHRISTIANS

Sometimes in a marriage, Christians marry people who are not Christians. This could cause a disruption of spiritual flow in a couple's life. The Christian might find himself or herself compromising their faith in God. In addition, the Christian and the non-Christian are going in different directions, spiritually. This is why Christians should marry Christians. In this way, the couple can focus on serving God and doing his will.

If both the husband and the wife are Christians, they can come together to pray to the Lord. Prayer keeps the marriage unified so that Satan won't try to break up the marriage. In fact, Christian couples should set aside some time for prayer and fasting. The apostle Paul says, "Defraud ye not one another, except it be with consent for a time, that ye may give yourselves to fasting and prayer; and come together again, that Satan tempt you not for your incontinency" (1 Cor. 7:5). Once a couple has ended the separation for fasting and praying, they need to come together and have normal sexual relationships. If they don't come together and continue to stay away from each other longer than expected, Satan will enter into the relationship and entice a couple's lack of control sexually, causing them to commit fornication or adultery.

The Christian couple must attend the same church to worship the Lord. It would not appear right for a husband and wife to go to different churches. Since they are serving the same God, they should worship Him together as a couple. But if a husband and wife attend different churches, they can't come together to serve the Lord. They might be exposed to different types of doctrines which may be contrary to God's word.

Christian couples must both have the Holy Spirit in their hearts. The Holy Spirit speaks to them and tells them how to govern their marriage according to God's will. But if only one person in the relationship has the Holy Spirit and the other doesn't have it, the Christian can win over their unsaved spouse to Christ (1 Cor. 7:14).

Keep in mind, the apostle Paul warns in 2 Corinthians 6:14 about mismatching with couples. He says, "Be ye not unequally yoked together with unbelievers; for what fellowship hath righteousness with unrighteousness? And what communion hath light with darkness?"

Christian couples can easily raise their children in a Christian environment. They can raise their children to accept Christ as the Lord and Savior of their lives. Children are taught to obey God's word and pray to Him. Proverbs 22:6 states, "Train up a child in a way he should go; and when he is old, he will not depart from it." Both parents must be involved in raising their children in a Christian environment. In order to do this, both parents must be Christians.

Unity in the home is important in a Christian marriage. In a Christian home, there should be some time set aside for daily devotions. The Bible needs to be the blueprint that the Christian family should live by in order to serve the Lord. In addition, praying as a family will tie the family together spiritually so that they could hear from God. Although a Christian doesn't have to marry a Christian (1 Cor. 7:12–13), it is best to strive for a Christian marriage because both the husband and the wife can be connected to God and instill Christian values in their children.

CHAPTER 16

GOD'S CHOICE IS THE BEST CHOICE

Some people believe that they can find the perfect mate for another individual. They would go as far as setting an individual up on a blind date. These people control individuals by telling them who can make them happy. But single Christians must beware of these people because they don't trust God's choice for them. God knows the mate a person should marry. When God makes a choice of a mate, He always makes the right choice.

In order for God to create a mate for a single Christian, he or she must allow Him to make the decision for him or her. He has a choice that is fitting and proper for single Christians. God will fix up a person for a single Christian. This person will bring happiness to a marital relationship because this person is God's choice, and He will never bless a single Christian with someone who is going to hurt him or her. In addition, God will bring a lifetime of commitment to the marriage. Just as Eve was created for Adam, God will create a mate for single Christians.

The single Christian needs to believe in God's choice for him or her. The Holy Spirit leads a single Christian to their right mate. The apostle Paul says, "If we live in the Spirit, let us also walk in the Spirit" (Gal. 5:25). The single Christian shouldn't have any doubt about God's choice for a mate because doubt always destroys faith. Faith overcomes doubt by helping the believer stand on a sure foundation that is Jesus Christ. If a single Christian abides in Jesus Christ, anything is possible for him or her.

God understands every human being he has created. He knows an individual's strengths and weaknesses. Because God knows these things, a single Christian can humble himself or herself before God. Humility allows God to work in his believers' life to find a mate. James 4:10 says, "Humble yourselves in the sight of the Lord, and He shall lift you up." God exalts his people by His power in due time so that they can rely on Him blessing them with a mate.

Single Christians should always seek God's will for the type of mate God wants them to have. Believers need to seek not what they want in a mate, but what God wants in a mate. What a single Christian may want in a mate may or may not be what God desires for him or her. The potential mate must have God's approval. Jesus says in Matthew 7:7–8, "Ask, and it shall be given you; seek, and you; seek, and ye shall find; knock, and it shall be opened unto you: For every one that asketh receiveth, and He that seeketh findeth; and to Him that knocketh, it shall be opened." Depending on God is best when looking for a husband or a wife.

When God choses a husband or a wife for a single Christian, he or she should praise God for his or her blessing that He has given to him or her. It was God who provided the mate for them. A single Christian shows gratitude to God for his blessing, or he or she wouldn't enjoy his or her blessings. When it comes down to being blessed with a mate, God deserves the praise and worship for His guidance from the single Christians. He knows what is best for His people.

A single Christian needs to declare that God's choice is the best choice. God uses a single Christian to lead him or her to the right mate. Serving the Lord guarantees a single Christian a chance to be blessed with a husband or a wife. The Lord believes in a lifetime commitment in a marriage. If a believer wants a good husband or wife, then the person must allow God to make the choice for him or her.

CHAPTER 17

DON'T GET IN GOD'S WAY

God has a special plan for all believers who desire to get married. Although He hasn't revealed His plan to them, believers are still supposed to maintain their faith to Him so that they can focus on His will. God's plan is usually predestined before a person is born. He will see to it that he follows through with his special plan, but sometimes, believers find themselves getting in God's way when looking for a mate. They may want a mate who is the total opposite of God's will. The Holy Spirit leads believers so that they will avoid getting in God's way.

Single Christians may get rushed into finding the right mate. They are currently living in a world that will probably rush single Christians into relationships so much that they won't take the time to consult God to see if this is the right mate according to His will. As a result, these single Christians end up getting hurt by individuals who they thought cared about them but didn't. However, single Christians need to open up their hearts to the Lord so that God can enter and reveal his will. They should slow down and let God work in creating a mate for them.

In addition, single Christians are precious in God's sight. He will keep them as a sheep being kept by a shepherd. As long as they are in this world, God will protect them from any hurt, harm, or danger. Satan may try to discourage a marriage from a lifetime commitment, but God puts his power in that marriage so that Satan won't break it up.

God's way of blessing a person with a mate may appear to be strong to a believer. This may cause the believer to be confused about how God will bless them with a mate. The believer may end up going in a direction that God didn't intend for them to go. Isaiah prophesied, "For my thoughts are not your thoughts, neither are your ways my ways, saith the Lord" (Isa. 55:8). A single Christian aligns their thoughts and their ways by reading and obeying God's word.

When a single Christian doesn't understand God, they can ask God for guidance, and God will clearly reveal his will.

Also, a single Christian needs to know that God considers time differently from man. When God looks at the time, he works according to his timetable, not man's. Sometimes, believers rush God if they assume he doesn't hear them or is taking a slow time answering prayers. Moses prayed of God, "For a thousand years in thy sight are but yesterday when it is past, and as a watch in the night" (Ps. 90:4). Believers should strive to know God's timing in their lives through the Holy Spirit who gives the believer the understanding they need to know about God's timing.

Single Christians can make the choice to get in God's way, but God's will never fail in a believer's life. God is always victorious in accomplishing His will. Believers must humble themselves before God and allow him to seek the right mate for them. God wants believers to seek him because He knows what is best for them. God is a good provider and cares about finding the right mate for His people.

CHAPTER 18

DON'T JUDGE THE BOOK
BY THE COVER

As a single Christian looks for the right mate to marry, he or she may look at the physical appearance of an individual. This person may have a handsome face or a well-conditioned body. In addition, the individual could speak kind words to a single Christian, but these words might be used to deceive that Christian. In reality the individual may have ill will toward the single Christian. But single Christians need not worry about going through these heartaches. God will surely bless them with a mate who can positively treat them well.

Single Christians must realize that looks can be deceiving. A person may appear to look good on the outside, but their inner spirit could be evil. The heart of an individual plays a major impact on who a person really is inside his or her heart. The heart opens up inside a single Christian who chooses to allow God to come in and take residence. The Holy Spirit works in the hearts of believers to them to the right mate. Believers shouldn't go by looks alone when looking for a mate.

A single Christian knows the heart of another person based on what he or she says out of his or her mouth. When a person says something out of his or her mouth, it comes from his or her heart. If people have an evil heart, then their hearts are unclean.

Jesus says, "But those things which proceed out of the mouth come forth from the heart; and they defile the man, for out of the heart proceed evil thoughts, murders, adulteries, fornications, thefts, false witness, blasphemies" (Matt. 15:18–19). Also, Jesus said, "For out of the abundance of the heart the mouth speaketh" (Matt. 12:34). A potential mate could be telling lies about himself or herself. He or she does this by trying to take the innocence of an individual. Single Christians are sometimes tricked into believing that this is the right mate for them. But these individuals could be described as "wolf in sheep's clothing." Jesus says, "Beware of false prophets which come to you in sheep's clothing, but inwardly they are ravening wolves" (Matt. 7:15). Single Christians must exercise caution when a potential mate approaches them or when they search for them. Whereas men search for the women, the women wait for the men to approach them.

Proverbs 18:22 states, "Whoso findeth a wife findeth a good thing, and obtaineth favor of the Lord." The man searches for his wife because he is going to be the head of the household just as Christ is the head of the church (Eph. 5:23). When the man approaches the woman, she should allow the Holy Spirit to help her decide if this man is going to be her husband. A man searching for a wife is a lot more serious than a man looking for a girlfriend because when a man is looking for a wife, he is looking for someone to have a lifetime commitment with him.

A single Christian's heart will demonstrate certain characteristics through the workings of the Holy Spirit. When the Holy Spirit works in the believer's life, there are certain outcomes that should be seen by other people. These elements will manifest themselves publicly for the entire world to see. Jesus says, "Either make the tree good and his fruit good; or else make the tree corrupt and his fruit corrupt; for the tree is known by its fruit" (Matt 12:33). The fruit in the scripture is the outcomes or results of a true Christian. The Apostle Paul mentions these outcomes or results as the fruit of the Holy Spirit. He states, "But the fruit of the spirit is love, joy, peace longsuffering, gentleness, goodness, faith, meekness, temperance, against such there is no law" (Gal.

5:22–23). If a single Christian is looking for a husband or a wife who is a Christian, these are the qualities he or she should find in him or her.

By God's guidance through the Holy Spirit, a single Christian won't have to worry about looking at the outside characteristics of an individual. He or she must be sensitive to the leading of the Holy Spirit as the Spirit speaks to him or her. The Apostle Paul says, "If ye live in the Spirit, let us also walk in the Spirit" (Gal. 5:20). Walking in the spirit means to live in the spirit who resides in the hearts of believers. Believers are to live in the freedom given to them by Jesus Christ. The apostle Paul says, "For, brethren, ye have been called unto liberty; only use not liberty for an occasion to the flesh, but by love serve one another" (Gal. 5:13).

Along with the Holy Spirit, single Christians must have faith in God. By having faith in God, He will reveal His will, and by his power, He will not allow Satan to deceive His people. Saints need to trust God by reading his word every day and obeying it. The apostle Paul told Timothy, "Study to show thyself approved unto God, a workmen that needth not to be ashamed, rightly dividing the word of truth" (2 Tim. 2:15). He also said in 2 Corinthians 5:7, "For we walk by faith, not by sight."

CHAPTER 19

GOD LOVES THE SINGLE PARENT

Single parents need to be loved by a companion. Sometimes, single parents may feel that they are alone in this world. They find themselves raising children by themselves without any assistance from the other parent. They want a mother or father figure for their child. But single parents shouldn't believe that they are alone because God will provide for these parents the help they need to raise their children. Single parents who are Christians must be careful of whom they would marry and allow to come in their lives and their children's lives.

Hagar, Sarah's handmaid, is a good example of a single parent. She became a single parent when Abraham got her pregnant in order for Sarah to have children through her because Sarah was barren. Sarah became angry with Hagar as she conceived and put her out of her house along with her son. But the angel of the Lord said of Hagar's son, Ishmael, "I will multiply thy seed exceedingly, that it shall not be numbered for multitude" (Gen. 16:10). Ishmael will be a descendant of the Arabic nation.

Like Hagar, God has a plan for a single parent's children. He will not allow single parents to raise children by themselves. He will be in their lives, instructing them on how to nurture their children. God loves the children of a single parent. When Hagar had her son, Sarah decided to put them out so that her son won't get an inheritance from Abraham and Sarah's son, Isaac. Before she left, Abraham gave her bread and water when God told him that Ishmael was going to be a great nation. As Hagar left, the water was spent and, her child started crying. Genesis 21:17 states "And God heard the voice of the lad; and the angel of God called to Hagar out of heaven, and said unto her, what aileth thee, Hagar? fear not; for God hath heard the voice of the lad, where he is." Also, God told Hagar, "Arise lift up the lad, and hold him in thine hand; for I will make him a great nation" (Gen 21:18). Jesus also loves children that he says,

"Suffer little children, and forbid them not, to come unto me; for of such is the kingdom of heaven" (Matt 19:14).

Single parents may desire to get married to someone who is a potential stepparent. These biological parents must let the potential stepparent know that what they are getting is a package deal. Not only does the potential stepparent show love to the biological parent, but also the potential stepparent must show love to the child. By showing love to both the parent and child, the relationship will run smoothly without any disputes. This will be beneficial to the child to see their biological parents get along with their stepparents because if the stepparents and biological parents are happy, the children will be happy too.

Even though the biological parents are separated or divorced and marry other people, the biological parents and stepparents can build a village around the children. This will ensure that the children will have a good success rate in life. Both the biological parents and the stepparents can bring some qualities for the children's well-being, such as a talent or skill. A biological parent should never disown his or her child. Regardless of whom the biological parents reconnect with in a relationship; he or she still has a spiritual connection to his or her child. This bond should never disappear from the child's life so that they would know who their real parents are.

Sometimes, when some people think of single parents, they automatically identify the mother as that single parent. Mothers do the bulk of the work, caring for the child, while the fathers pay child support. But what most people must realize is that there are single fathers in our society, as well as single mothers. God is no respect of persons to any single parent whether it be a single mother or a single father. He will help these single parents nurture their children in these trying times in this world.

In the meantime, the biological parents need to have a civil relationship with each other for the child's sake. The child shouldn't ever see his or her parents arguing or insulting one another. Both parents must act in the best interest of the child. When the father pays his child support, the mother needs to use the money to care for the child, not spend the child support on herself. Child support should never be confused with spousal support. Fathers shouldn't be deadbeats and sperm donors to their children; they should be setting examples in their children's lives to be a strong presence to them.

CHAPTER 20

CONCLUSION

The most important decision a single person could make is deciding to accept Jesus Christ as Lord and Savior of his or her life. While the world may be pressuring them to get married, Jesus Christ gave himself to the world so that the world through Him may be saved.

The issue is not whether to stay single or get married; the issue is whether a soul of a person is going to end up in heaven or hell. At some point in time, everyone is going to leave this world to stand before the judgment seat of God to receive punishment or a reward of eternal life.

The good news is there is still time to accept Christ as Lord and Savior. Jesus has his arm open wide to the sinners. He wishes that none should perish but everyone should receive salvation for their sins.

The world could come to an end any day now. The Lord describes his coming as a "thief in the night." The signs are there to indicate the world's end. Therefore, people must get ready to meet the Lord. This world is not our home; it is only our temporary residence.

You, the reader, can accept Christ by faith right now regardless of your marital status. Your marital status is not going to save you. You can only be saved by the powerful and cleansing blood of Jesus Christ.

If you would like to accept Jesus Christ as your Lord and Savior, pray this prayer with me by faith: Lord Jesus, forgive me for my sins that I committed. Wash me clean so I can serve you. I place my trust in you to save me from my sins. I believe you arose again from the dead. My life belongs to you, and I will serve you all the days of my life. May your precious Holy Spirit live in me to guide me and obey your will. And from this moment on, I will love you and serve you all the days of my life.

If you prayed this prayer, congratulations! You have taken the initial step to be saved. Now you are a part of the body of Christ. Next, you have to find a local church to praise and worship God with other believers. Ask God's Holy Spirit to lead you to the right church. Read and study your Bible everyday. Develop a prayer life for daily devotion.

Being single or getting married is not an easy task. God must be present in either marital status in order for a single Christian to function spiritually.

Regardless of whether you decide to be single or get married, remember: as Christian music artist Tom Green, the host of Christian Music Video Show *Light Music* would say, "God loves you, and He has a wonderful plan for your life."

ABOUT THE AUTHOR

Wayne Drayton is a born again Christian who has decided to live a single life for the Lord since 1996. He encourages Christians to realize that a person doesn't have to please God by getting married. They should please him by having faith in God. In addition, if a Christian wants to get married, he or she should marry the person God has ordained for him or her.

Drayton currently serves as a church deacon at Biblical House of God in North Charleston, South Carolina. He is also a faithful Sunday school teacher who enjoys encouraging his church with the Word of God every Sunday morning. Drayton also believes that God can help a single Christian maintain a single life or bless a Christian with a mate of his choosing. Hence, the name of his book, *The Two Side of Being Single: A Biblical Perspective*. Drayton sincerely hopes his book would enlighten single Christians to trust God whether they choose to stay single or get married.

www.ingramcontent.com/pod-product-compliance
Lightning Source LLC
Chambersburg PA
CBHW070942120626
46546CB00004B/1527